BONUS 40-SONG CD!

40 TRAVELING SONGS FOR HOURS OF IN-CAR FUN!

Message to Parents: Turning "Travel Time" into "Bible Time" is the idea behind The Ultimate TRAVEL TIME Bible! Let's face it, you and your kids spend a lot of time in the car traveling to soccer practice, dance class, and school functions. So why not pop in the 40-song Bible CD and listen to great Scripture songs they'll enjoy and remember! Plus they can do one of a hundred different activities in the accompanying activity pad. Best of all, they'll enjoy reading about Noah's Ark, Jonah and the Whale, Ruth, David and Goliath, Daniel and the Lions, and the story of Jesus—all in one great Travel Time Anytime Bible Story Collection! It's a lot of FUN and builds a lot of FAITH. My Travel Time Bible! ENJOY!

The Ultimate TRAVEL TIME BIBLE

b&h Kids

B&H Publishing Group, Nashville, Tennessee
BHPublishingGroup.com

Text copyright © 2007 by Stephen Elkins

Illustrations by Jim Conaway

Cover and interior design by Chad Stephens & Jay Elkins
Nashville, Tennessee

ISBN: 0-8054-2647-7
ISBN-13: 978-0-8054-2647-2

Published by B&H Publishing Group
Nashville, Tennessee

All rights reserved. Printed in China.

220.95
Bible Stories
Verses used are paraphrases from various Bible translations.

All songs (except Public Domain) written & arranged by Stephen Elkins
Copyright © 2007 by Wonder Workshop, Inc.
Nashville, Tennessee
All rights reserved. Unauthorized duplication of CD prohibited by law.

1 2 3 4 5   11 10 09 08 07

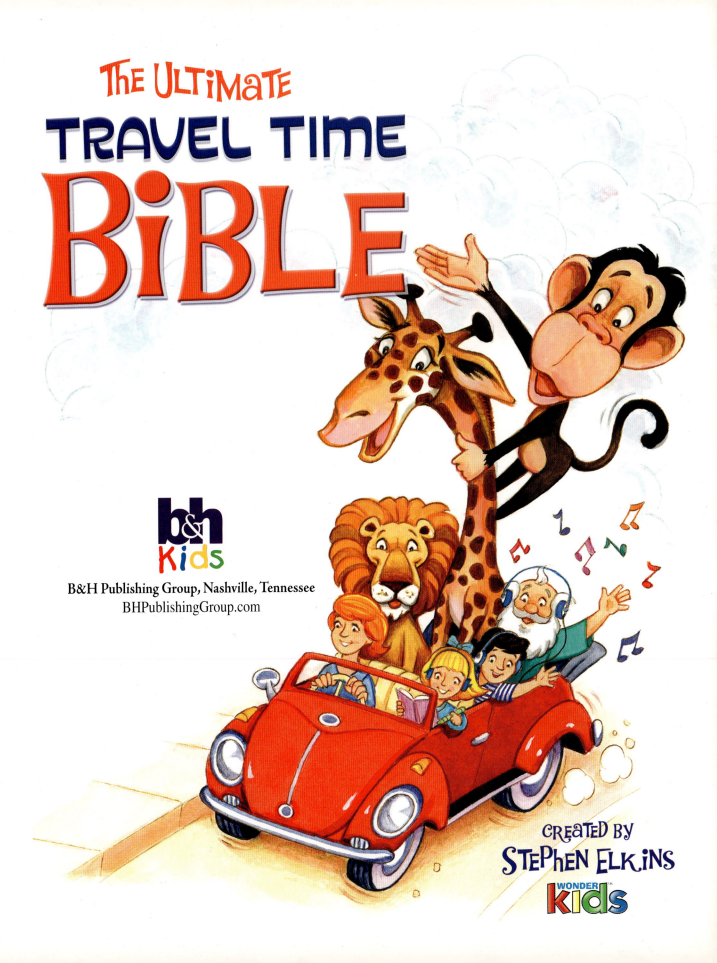

The Ultimate
TRAVEL TIME
BIBLE

B&H Kids

B&H Publishing Group, Nashville, Tennessee
BHPublishingGroup.com

CREATED BY
STEPHEN ELKINS

Wonder Kids

The Ultimate Travel Time Bible

PRESENTED TO:

_____

FROM:

_____

The Creation
I will remember my Creator

Before anyone or anything traveled anyplace or anywhere, God was busy creating! The book of Genesis tells us that God created everyone and everything in seven days.

On the first day, he created light.
On the second day, he created the sky.
On the third day, God made dry land appear.

On the fourth day, he created the sun, the moon, and all the stars.

On the fifth day, God created every kind of bird and fish.

On the sixth day, God made all of the animals, big and small. But he wasn't done yet!

He made Adam and Eve, the first man and woman. Now there was someone to see all that God had made.

Then on the seventh day, God rested. And that's what we should do, too!

Travel Game #1

21 Questions

Think of an animal found in the Bible and write it down.
(Don't worry, they were all on Noah's Ark!)
Other players start asking questions about the animal.
The answer must be either "yes" or "no."
For example:
You CAN ask, "Does your animal have stripes?"
You CANNOT ask, "What color is your animal?"
You can ask a maximum of 21 questions.

Have fun guessing the animals!

In the Beginning
CD Track 1

Genesis (Genesis)
Verse one-one (verse one-one)
In the beginning God created
The heavens and the earth.

Day 1, he made the light.
Darkness did abound.
He called it day, and by the way,
No earth was spinning 'round.
Day 2, he made the waters.
It's enough to laugh.
I'm reminded every time
I have to take a bath.

Genesis (Genesis)
Verse one-one (verse one-one)
In the beginning God created
The heavens and the earth.

Day 3, guess what he made.
Sailors shout hooray!
The seven seas all came to be
On that special day.
Day 4, he made the star shine,
The sun and moon above.
In heaven's light on starry nights
I see our Father's love.

Day 5, he made the sparrows
And every bird that flies,
And all the creatures in the sea,
God made them on day five.
Day 6, he made the animals
Both big and small, you see.
And on that day (hip-hip-hooray)
God made Adam and Eve.

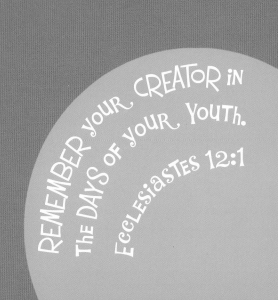

REMEMBER your CREATOR in The DAYS of your Youth.
Ecclesiastes 12:1

ADAM & EVE
I will praise God for His goodness

Everything God made was good. But there was one special place beyond compare. It was called the Garden of Eden. And like any good father, God wanted Adam and Eve to be happy and safe.

So he gave them a single warning, "Do not eat the fruit of the Tree of Good and Evil. If you do, you will die."

Adam and Eve obeyed God. Then one day a crafty being spoke to Eve. He was beautiful and seemed very wise. "God doesn't want you to know what he knows." He was telling lies about God.

"That's why he made that silly rule. Go ahead and eat the fruit. You won't die."

But Eve did not know it was that ol' serpent, the Devil. Eve thought, "Maybe he's right. Why can't I know what God knows?" So she ate the fruit and gave some to Adam.

Soon they heard God say, "You have disobeyed." Adam and Eve were sorry for what they had done. Eden was no longer perfect. Sin had come in. It was a very sad day!

Travel Game #2

Eden, A to Z

Imagine you're in the Garden of Eden!
What do you see?
The first player begins with the letter A.
"Adam saw an Apple."
The next player repeats what the first player said,
but adds something that begins with the letter "B."
"Adam saw an Apple and a Banana."
The third player adds something that begins
with the letter "C" and so on.
Let's go A to Z!

Can you remember all of the things that Adam saw?

"ADAM SAW AN APPLE AND A BANANA"

I Am Wonderfully Made
CD Track 2

I praise you because
I am fearfully and wonderfully made.
I praise you because
I am fearfully and wonderfully made.

I am a miracle heaven has made,
Glorious miracle.
That's why I praise my Father in heaven
For all the great things he has done.

I praise you because
I am fearfully and wonderfully made.
I praise you because
I am fearfully and wonderfully made.

My voice is singing praises to God.
My heart is filled with the joy of the Lord,
And that's why I'm singing.
Lord, there is none like you.

Praise the Lord, for the Lord is good.
Psalm 135:3

Noah's Ark
I will recall God's promises

Did you know that God can speak through a rainbow? Long ago, all the people on the earth decided they didn't need God. His commands were just getting in the way of their fun. So everyone ignored God. Everyone, that is, except for Noah and his family.

Noah was different, and it's hard to be different. It's hard to love and serve God when others don't. But Noah did!

One day, God spoke to Noah. He told Noah to build a giant boat. He would soon send a great flood to cover the entire earth.

Only Noah and his family would be saved. There was, however, another small detail. This giant boat would be full of animals: two of every kind. They were going on the trip with Noah.

Noah cut wood, hammered nails, and built a boat. With all on board, the rain started to fall. The earth was flooded. All was washed away. But soon the sun dried the land, and Noah and the animals came out of the ark.

God placed a rainbow in the sky to say, "I love you. And I promise to never flood the whole earth again."

What a beautiful rainbow!

Travel Game #3
Livin' on the Ark

Player 1—think of an animal you'd like to be.
Then, on the count of three,
pretend to BE that animal!
Now it's time to guess the animal.
Everybody guesses.
The first one who guesses correctly wins the round!
Keep playing until you've pretended to be
every animal that was on the ark!

How many animals have you been today?

Rainbows
CD Track 3

I have set my rainbow in the clouds,
And it will be a sign, colorful sign.
I have set my rainbow in the sky.
A promise I make to you, here's why—
Never again will waters rise,
For I have set my rainbow in the sky!

Reds and violet, greens and blues,
Colorful promise I give to you.
A promise I made, a promise I'll keep.
So rest, dear child—sleep, sleep, sleep.

The Lord is faithful to all of His promises.
Psalm 145:13

Joseph's Coat
All things work together for good

Jacob had a favorite son named Joseph. Jacob gave Joseph a very special coat made of fine cloth of many colors. It was fit for a king. Of course, this made Joseph's brothers very jealous. They decided to get rid of Joseph!

One day, a caravan of Egyptian merchants passed by. Joseph was sold by his own brothers to the merchants. He was now a slave and on his way to Egypt.

His brothers covered Joseph's coat with blood. They lied to Jacob, saying Joseph had been killed by a wild animal. Jacob mourned.

But, don't worry. All things were working together for good! Joseph found favor with the king of Egypt. He was made second in command of the nation.

Once again, he wore a royal coat of many colors. God told Joseph that a seven-year famine was coming. So Joseph stored up grain. One day, Joseph's brothers came to Egypt to buy food.

They stood before Joseph, but they did not recognize him. When they did, they feared Joseph would be angry. But Joseph said, "What you meant for evil, God meant for good." It was a happy reunion day!

Travel Game #4

Stories by Us!

Are you ready to make up a funny story?
The first player begins a story,
"On the road to Egypt I passed a camel named..."
From this point on, the player must add to the story
until your car passes a billboard.
The next player picks up the story where the first player left off.
That player continues the story until the next
billboard is passed, and so on.
The game goes on until somebody can't continue the story, or until
everyone is bent over laughing, whichever comes first!

Are you laughing yet?

Brother, Where Art Thou
CD Track 4

O, brother where art thou, where have you gone?
I'm far away in Egypt, 'cause you treated me wrong.
O, brother where art thou, where have you been?
Far away in Egypt land working for the king.

You intended to harm me,
But God intended it for good.
You intended to harm me,
But God had a plan for this brotherhood.

O, brother where art thou, where have you gone?
I'm far away in Egypt, 'cause you treated me wrong.
O, brother where art thou, where have you been?
Far away in Egypt land working for the king.

To accomplish what is now being done,
Our God, He is so wise.
To accomplish what is now
The saving of many, so many lives.

All things work together for good for those who love God.
Romans 8:28

Moses' Burning Bush
I know that God can do all things

Can God do some things, or can God do all things? Moses believed that God could do all things . . . all things except use him to free God's people. But he soon changed his mind.

One day, Moses was tending his sheep near Mount Horeb. Suddenly, he saw a bush that was on fire, but it did not burn up. Then, to his amazement, a voice came from the bush: "I have heard the cries of my people, Moses."

The voice kept on. "I am sending you to Egypt to free them. You will lead them to the Promised Land."

Moses realized it was the voice of God. He answered, "O Lord, I really don't speak very well. Why don't you send someone else?" Moses believed God could do all things . . . all things except use him. But God did use Moses to free his people. For all things are possible with God.

Travel Game #5

Oops Words

Each person in the car writes down one word found in the Bible. It can be any word.
These words are written down and become the "OOPS" words for the trip.
If someone uses your "oops" word, you get a point.
The winner is the one with the <u>most</u> points after a certain amount of time (30 minute minimum).

Don't say the wrong thing!

When I Am Afraid
CD Track 5

When I am afraid,
I will trust in you.
I will trust in you, my Father.
When I am afraid,
I will trust in you.
I will trust in you,
O Lord my God.

No situation, no aggravation
Is beyond my Lord, my Lord.
In my confusion,
The real solution
Is trusting in his holy Word.

When I am afraid,
I will trust in you
I will trust in you, my Father.
When I am afraid,
I will trust in you.
I will trust in you,
O Lord my God.

No circumstances,
When fear advances,
Call upon the Lord.
He's like a father, like no other.
Keep trusting in his holy Word.

When I am afraid,
I will trust in you.
I will trust in you, my Father.
When I am afraid,
I will trust in you.
I will trust in you,
O Lord my God.

With God, all things are possible. Matthew 19:26

The Red Sea Miracle
I Will Commit my Way to the Lord

Sometimes we may not know the way to go. But God always knows the way. Take the case of Moses. Moses stood before the king of Egypt and delivered God's message, "Let my people go!" Finally, after horrible plagues of frogs, flies, gnats, hailstorms, locusts, darkness, and diseases—even death—the king let the people of Israel go free!

But the king changed his mind. "Let's go get the Israelites and bring them back." Meanwhile, Moses and all the people were camped by the Red Sea. Suddenly, everyone saw the army coming to capture them. "What can we do?" they shouted.

The Egyptian army was thundering toward them, and the Red Sea was behind them. There was no escape!

Then Moses said, "Behold the power of God." The Red Sea parted and before them was a highway right through the middle of the sea. It was a miracle!

All the people passed through the water safely. But when the king's army tried to pass, the water closed in on them. Yes, God's timing is always right. He makes a way when there's no way at all!

Travel Game #6
Red, Yellow, Green

We are going to look for objects that are one of three colors: red, yellow, or green. These are the colors of a stop light. The driver of the car will call out what color to look for between stop lights. Then, everyone has to find as many things outside the car as they can that match the color the driver called out. Everyone must call out things they see. Each item may only be counted once. The game doesn't end until you've reached the next stop light.

How many colored things did you see?

I Will Sing to the Lord
CD Track 6

I will sing to the Lord, O-oh,
I will sing to the Lord, O-oh,
I will sing to the Lord for he is highly exalted.
I will sing to the Lord, O-oh,
I will sing to the Lord, O-oh,
I will sing to the Lord for he is good!

The horse and its rider he has hurled into the sea.
The horse and its rider he has hurled into the sea.
Splish, splash the waters did crash,
Down on Pharaoh in a flash!
The horse and rider hurled into the sea.

The Lord is my strength and my song, I praise his name.
The Lord is my strength and my song, I praise his name.
Praise, praise, oh I will raise
To my Savior all my days!
The Lord forever is my strength and song!

Commit your way to the Lord.
Psalm 37:5

Samson's Strength

God is the source of my strength

What is the source of our strength? Samson found out the hard way! Samson was the strongest man who ever lived. He once defeated a lion with his bare hands. What was his secret? From birth, Samson had been set apart to do the work of the Lord.

God told him to never cut his hair. As long as Samson obeyed, he would be strong.

Samson had a girlfriend named Delilah. But she wasn't much of a friend at all. She was a traitor! She was paid lots of money to find out the source of Samson's strength. She asked Samson, again and again, "What makes you so strong?"

But Samson would not tell her. Then one night, Samson said, "My hair has never been cut. If my hair were cut, I would be as weak as any other man." As he fell asleep, Samson's enemies cut his hair, tied him up, and took him away.

A long time later, Samson looked up to heaven and prayed, "O Lord, my God, strengthen me one last time." Samson gave a mighty push against the enemies' temple posts, and down came the building. Samson found his strength in obedience to God. That is the secret to being strong!

Travel Game #7

Samson's Adventures

Players will need two coins of any size.
Both coins are to be tossed at the start of each player's turn.
1 head, 1 tail: Player moves 1 space.
2 heads: Player moves 2 spaces
2 tails: Player moves 3 spaces.
Move around the game board on pages 30–31,
following the instructions printed in the boxes
(and answering the silly questions!)
The first one to complete the board wins!

Let's play a board game!

God Is Our Refuge and Strength
CD Track 7

God is our refuge and strength,
An ever present help in trouble.
God is our refuge and strength,
An ever present help in trouble.

Call upon the name of the Lord.
He will hear you, he will hear you.
Call upon the name of the Lord.
He is near you, it's oh so true!

God is our refuge and strength,
An ever present help in trouble.
God is our refuge and strength,
An ever present help in trouble.

Call upon the name of the Lord.
He will guide you, he will guide you.
Call upon the name of the Lord.
He'll walk beside you, it's oh so true!

God is our refuge and our strength.
Psalm 46:1

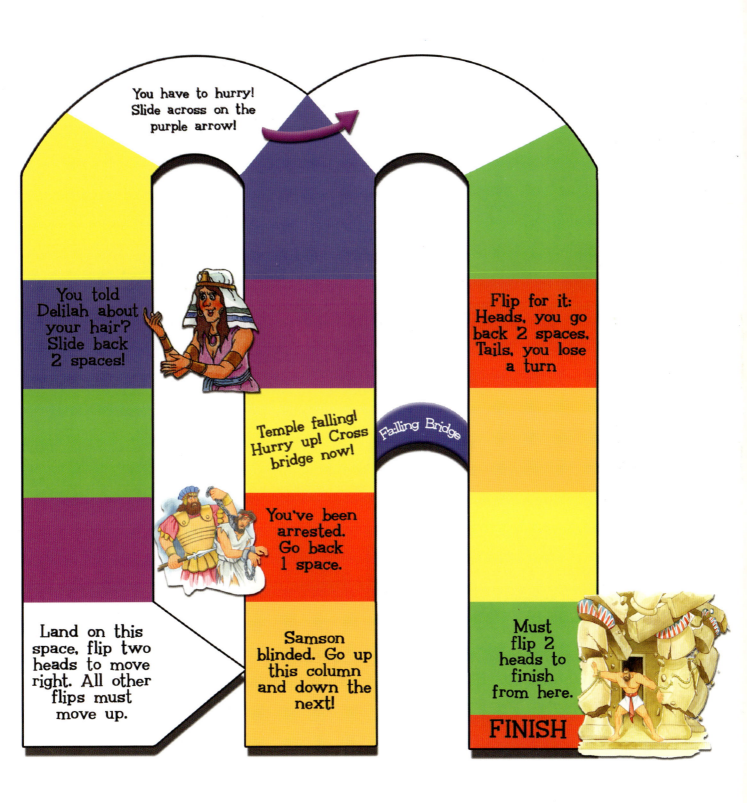

Ruth & Naomi
God will provide for me

When you let God provide, you're in for an amazing blessing, as Ruth discovered. Once, there was a famine in Judah. A woman named Naomi and her family traveled from Judah to a far away country called Moab. They went there to find food. In Moab, Naomi's two sons grew up and married Ruth and Orpah. They were very happy until both of Naomi's sons died. When Naomi learned the famine in Judah had ended, she decided to return home.

Orpah stayed in Moab. But Ruth said to Naomi, "Where you go, I will go. Your people will be my people, and your God, my God." So the two women traveled back to Judah.

Ruth worked in the field gathering grain. The field was owned by a good man named Boaz. Ruth and Boaz fell in love and were married. Though Ruth had given up much to help Naomi, her kindness was blessed. God provided Ruth with a home, a husband, a beautiful baby, and joy in her heart.

Travel Game #8
Smiley Face

The first player must begin by picking out a silly phrase. It can be anything at all. We like to start with: "The cat's tail."
Everyone, in no particular order, has to ask the first player a question. It can be any question at all.
The first player then has to answer every question with the funny phrase, but answer without smiling! Not even a grin!
A typical round would go something like this:

"What do you brush your teeth with?"   "The cat's tail."
"What is your favorite thing to eat?"   "The cat's tail."
"Where are you going on vacation?"   "The cat's tail."

See how many questions you can answer without smiling. The one who answers the most is the winner!

Where You Go
CD Track 8

Where you go, I will go.
Where you stay, I will stay.
And your people will be my people,
And your God will be my God.

Friends are friends eternally.
That's the way a friend should be,
Just like Ruth and Naomi.
Friends are friends eternally.
Friends are friends eternally.

Where you go, I will go.
Where you stay, I will stay.
And your people will be my people,
And your God will be my God.

The Lord will provide.
Genesis 22:14

David & Goliath

The name of the Lord is powerful

When we "come in the name of the Lord," we bring with us his power and might. David shows us a wonderful example of this truth.

David was a shepherd boy. One day, his father sent him to the battlefield to take food to his older brothers. They were fighting the Philistines. There he saw a giant named Goliath standing on the battlefield. He was making fun of Israel and mocking their God. David said to King Saul, "Do not fear this Philistine. I will go and fight him."

David gathered five stones and his slingshot and walked bravely toward Goliath. David said, "You come against me with a sword and spear, but I come against you in the name of the Lord!" David took out one stone and hurled it toward the giant. Down he went, and Goliath was defeated. The little shepherd boy had won the victory in the name of the Lord!

Travel Game #9
Travel Time Rhymes

Player 1 begins by saying a word.
It can be any word at all.
The next player must come up with a word
that rhymes with the first word.
Each player must say a word that rhymes with that word.
If a player cannot think of a word, he is out.
A round is over when no one else can think of a rhyming
word. The last one to rhyme receives one point.
The first player to 7 points wins!

Nothing rhymes with chimney, depth, month, orange, purple, or wasp!

Be Thou Exalted
CD Track 9

As I kneel before your presence,
I am filled with saving grace
That has echoed through the ages like a song.
And it tells the love of heaven
Reaching down to meet our need.
Oh, I thank you, Lord, for reaching down to me.

Be thou exalted,
Be thou exalted,
Be thou exalted, O God, above the earth.
Be thou exalted,
Be thou exalted, O Lord,
Be thou exalted, O God,
Exalted, O God,
Exalted above the earth.

PROCLAIM THE POWER OF GOD.
PSALM 68:34

Elijah's Test

I will serve the Lord

What does it mean "to serve"? That's easy! It means we focus our attention on someone else's needs and not our own. Elijah served the living God. But others like Ahab and Jezebel served Baal, a false god. Ahab blamed Elijah for all of Israel's trouble.

But Elijah said, "No, not I, but you and your family have caused Israel's trouble by serving Baal. So call your priests and meet me on Mount Carmel."

Hundreds of priests of Baal came. But only Elijah stood for God. "Prepare two bulls and lay them on the altars," Elijah said.

"Call on your god and I alone will call on mine. The god who answers with fire from heaven is the one true God." They all agreed. Baal did not answer. But God sent a blazing fire from heaven, burning the sacrifice, the wood, and even the stones! Elijah served the one true God. Let's serve him, too!

Travel Game #10
The Spelling Test

Open this book to any page.
You have 10 seconds to pick out a word on that page.
Ask the person next to you to spell it.
If he or she spells it correctly, then they are in.
If they misspell it, they are out.
Pass the book to the player who correctly spelled the word. That player then has 10 seconds to pick a word.
The next player then has to spell it, and so on.

Who is the spelling champ?

Glorify the Lord with Me
CD Track 10

Glorify, glorify the Lord with me!
Glorify, glorify the Lord with me!
Let us exalt his name together.
Let us exalt his name forever.
Glorify, glorify the Lord with me!
Glorify the Lord, our Lord.

In everything you say, glorify the Lord.
Every night and day, glorify the Lord.
In all that you do, let his glory show through.
Glorify the Lord with me!

Glorify, glorify the Lord with me!
Glorify, glorify the Lord with me!
Let us exalt his name together.
Let us exalt his name forever.
Glorify, glorify the Lord with me!
Glorify the Lord, our Lord.

Serve the Lord with gladness.
Psalm 100:2

The 8 Year Old King
I can make a difference

Are we ever too young to serve the Lord? Josiah was only eight years old when he became king. Yet at such an early age, he loved the Lord with all his heart. He sought to please him in every way. God did not want his people to worship idols. So Josiah had all the idols of Judah destroyed. Then he sent men to repair the temple of God.

While the men were working, they found a great treasure! It was the book of the law written by Moses. It had been lost for many years.

How excited Josiah was! He called all the people together and read the law. There was a great celebration in the kingdom.

Though he was only eight years old, Josiah served the Lord faithfully and made a difference in his world. We can, too!

Travel Game #11
The Rule of 8

First, each player must choose a color.
Players must then find 8 cars as they drive along
that are the color they picked.
The first player to find 8 cars of his or her color receives 1 point.
Players then choose different colors.
No player is allowed to have the same color
twice until everyone else has had it.
A second round is played, then a third, etc.
The first person to get to 8 points is the winner!

Who is the ruler of "The Rule of 8?"

Because You Are Young
CD Track 11

Don't let anyone
Don't let anyone
Look down on you.
Don't let anyone
Don't let anyone
Look down on you
Because, because, because you are young.
No! Don't let anyone
Don't let anyone
Look down on you.

Set an example for believers in life.
Set an example for believers in love.
Set an example for believers in faith.
And don't let anyone
No, not anyone
Look down on you.

Don't let anyone look down on you because you are young. 1 Timothy 4:12

QUEEN ESTHER
When I'm afraid, I will trust in God

Sometimes we think that people who show great courage have no fear. Not so! Many times people show courage in spite of their fears, like Esther did. She was queen of Persia. Esther was Jewish, but she told no one. She had a cousin named Mordecai who loved her like his own daughter.

Haman was a very proud man who served the king. Everyone bowed before him—everyone but Mordecai. He would bow to no one but God. This made Haman very angry. So he planned to kill all of the Jews. When Mordecai heard about Haman's evil plan, he told Esther. But according to the law, Esther could not go to the king.

So the Jews gathered and prayed. Then Esther went in to see the king. She could have been killed for breaking the law. She told the king that Haman was planning to kill all of the Jews, and that she was Jewish. Because of her courage, the Jews were saved.

Esther conquered her fears by committing them to God. We can too!

Travel Game #12

Esther's Plates

Each player needs a piece of paper and a pencil or pen.
Each player writes the words "Queen Esther" on their paper.
Each player must spell out "Queen Esther" from
letters seen on the license plates of passing cars.
Mark off each letter as you see it,
calling it out loud as you mark it off.
But a car's plate can only be used once for each letter on it.
So if the plate reads "QTR-876," only one "Q," "T," and "R" can be
used between all players. The first person to call it out marks it off.
The winner is the first one to mark off each letter.
Try using other Bible characters' names!

Keep watching for Queen Esther!

How Excellent Is Thy Name
CD Track 12

O Lord, our Lord,
How excellent is thy name in all the earth, we sing.
Lord, our Lord,
How excellent is thy name in all the earth, we sing.
Praises, your praises,
O Lord, we sing your wondrous praise!
Praises, your praises,
O Lord, we sing your wondrous praise!

O Lord, our Lord,
How excellent is thy name in all the earth, we sing.
Lord, our Lord,
How excellent is thy name in all the earth, we sing.
Praises, your praises,
O Lord, we sing your wondrous praise!
Praises, your praises,
O Lord, we sing your wondrous praise!

Do not fear, for I am with you.
Isaiah 41:10

The Fiery Furnace

I will try to please the Lord in all I do

If I don't do what my friends do, they might laugh at me. But if I do it just to keep them from laughing, my father and mother will be disappointed in me. Shadrach, Meshach, and Abednego had to make a choice like that. King Nebuchadnezzar had built an idol. He surrounded the idol with a host of musicians. When the music played, everyone was to bow and worship the idol.

The king was pleased until Shadrach, Meshach, and Abednego made their choice. They refused to bow. Did I tell you the penalty for not bowing to the idol was death? The king had a fiery, red-hot furnace burning for people who didn't obey him. But Shadrach, Meshach, and Abednego desired to please God more than they desired to please the king. So the king had them thrown into the fiery furnace!

But suddenly everyone saw four men in the fire! Jesus had saved them! We, too, must do what pleases our heavenly Father, regardless of what our friends may say! You will be blessed if you do!

Travel Game #13

Be a Hero

There are 40 Bible characters listed on the bottom of this page. This game starts with the first player choosing one of those characters. Don't tell anyone who you chose!
Then, take turns acting like the character you picked.
The first one to correctly guess which character you're pretending to be gets one point.
The first person to get 3 points is the winner.

Which Bible character are you going to be?

Adam	Joshua	David	Gabriel
Eve	Samson	Goliath	Peter
The Serpent	Delilah	Josiah	James
Noah	Elijah	Shadrach	John
Moses	Job	Daniel	Prodigal Son
Jacob	Esther	A Lion	Lost Sheep
Joseph	Haman	Jonah	Good Samaritan
Abraham	Ruth	The Whale	Zacchaeus
Isaac	Naomi	Mary	Lazarus
Jacob	Samuel	Jesus	Paul

The Plans I Have for You
CD Track 13

For I know the plans I have for you, my little children.
For I know your plans, declares the Lord.
For I know the plans I have for you, my little children.
For I know your plans, declares the Lord.

Plans to prosper you
And not to harm you (No!)
Plans to give you hope
And a future that will grow.

For I know the plans I have for you, my little children.
For I know your plans, declares the Lord.
For I know the plans I have for you, my little children.
For I know your plans, declares the Lord.

Then you will call upon me,
Come and pray to me (Me!)
And I will listen to you.
That's how it should be.

FiND OUT WHAT PLEASES THE LORD.
EPHESIANS 5:10

Daniel & The Lions
I will pray, no matter what

Daniel prayed, no matter what! Every morning, noon, and night, Daniel would open his window and pray his prayer of thanksgiving.

There were powerful men in the kingdom who wanted to get rid of Daniel. They were jealous of his power and position. Since they knew that Daniel prayed to God every day, they tricked the king into passing a really bad law. It was illegal now to pray to anyone except the king. Everyone stopped praying . . . everyone except Daniel. He kept praying, no matter what. Why would he keep on praying? He prayed because he had always prayed, even as a child.

When the jealous men saw Daniel praying, they had him arrested. The king had Daniel thrown into a den of hungry lions. Daniel was afraid, but he knew God was with him. When morning came, everyone saw Daniel was safe. The Lord had protected him. Yes, Daniel prayed, no matter what. We can be like Daniel!

Travel Game #14
Daniel Didn't Drive

This game is a tongue twister game!
Player 1 must come up with a phrase using words
that start with the first letter of his or her name.
For example, Jenny might say,
"Jenny jumped from a juniper tree in June."
Use the first letter of your name at least 4 times!
The other players do the same thing,
using the first letter of their names.

Figure out how fast you can say each phrase!

Adam ate an amazing amount of apples and announced that his appetite was absolutely absent.

Three Times a Day
CD Track 14

Three times a day
He got down on his knees!
(yeah, yeah)
Three times a day
He got down on his knees!
(yeah, yeah)
He got down and prayed and prayed,
Giving thanks to God, I say.
Three times a day Daniel prayed!
(yeah, yeah)

We should be praying
Every single day.
We should be staying on our knees,
O, hear me say:
"God is our helper
And it would be a shame
When lions gather 'round
Not to know his name."

Pray without ceasing.
1 Thessalonians 5:17

A Whale of a Tale
I will obey the Lord

A lot of bad stuff can happen when we choose to disobey God. Jonah can testify to this! God told Jonah to sail to a far away city called Nineveh. He was to tell the people to serve God. But instead of sailing to Nineveh, Jonah went in the opposite direction.

As he sailed away, there was a terrible storm. The ship was about to sink. Jonah knew God was angry and had caused the storm. "Throw me into the sea and the storm will stop," Jonah told the sailors.

"Splash!" went Jonah into the sea. Before he drowned, he was swallowed by a giant fish. There in the fish's belly, Jonah prayed. "I'm sorry, Lord. I should have obeyed you. I will do as you ask." Suddenly the fish burped, and Jonah landed on a sandy shore. He ran to Nineveh and preached to the people. Jonah saw the whole city come back to the Lord.

Travel Game #15

The Truth in the Tail

Three of the statements listed on this page are totally made up. Have a grown-up read all 18 sentences. Then every player should write down the number of the three "bogus" facts. (answers below)

1. All whales have two pectoral flippers for stopping and turning.
2. All whales have tail flukes, or a large tail fin for moving forward.
3. Whales breathe air.
4. A whale's nose is on top of its head.
5. A gray whale's blow hole is heart-shaped.
6. The largest of all whales is the blue whale, who is up to 90 feet long.
7. Dagger whales can live for up to 235 years.
8. Depending on the kind of toothed whale, it may eat fish, squid, crabs, shrimp, sea-stars, sharks, seals, sea lions, penguins, even other whales, dolphins, and porpoises.
9. Male humpback whales are known for their singing.
10. An adult gray whale eats about 660 pounds of food a day, or 340,000 pounds total during their 4-month polar feeding period.
11. In their first 8 months of life, baby blue whales gain 200 pounds a day.
12. Killer whales build traps out of seaweed to catch their food.
13. You can tell an adult male from a female killer whale by the shape of its dorsal fin.
14. Most whale species can't turn their heads.
15. Beluga whales can "make faces" with their flexible lips and forehead.
16. Springer whales play a game similar to basketball, called Majong.
17. People sometimes use whale blubber, or fat, to make perfume.
18. The bowhead whale has the most fat per body size.

answer: 7, 12, 16

Swim, Jonah, Swim
CD Track 15

Jonah 4:2—
You are a gracious and compassionate God,
Slow to anger and abounding in love.

You are a gracious and compassionate God.
(swim Jonah, swim)
You are a gracious and compassionate God.
(swim Jonah, swim)
Slow to anger, abounding in love,
Watching and guiding from heaven above.
O, you are a gracious and compassionate God.

You are a gracious and compassionate God.
(swim Jonah, swim)
You are a gracious and compassionate God.
In my distress I called to the Lord,
O, and he answered, of this I am sure.
O, you are a gracious and compassionate God.
(swim Jonah, swim)

To obey is better than to sacrifice. 1 Samuel 15:22

The Birth of Jesus

I will listen for God's voice

Did you ever wonder why angels announced the birth of Jesus to shepherds and not to kings?

The journey from Nazareth to Bethlehem had been hard and Mary was very tired. Joseph had tried to find a place to rest, but Bethlehem was crowded and there was no room in the inn. So Jesus was born in a humble stable with the cows and donkeys. The son of God slept in a manger.

All was quiet and still on the hillside as the shepherds watched their flock. Suddenly, the night was filled with the sound of angelic voices. The shepherds heard the message in their song. Christ the Lord is born! Wise men brought the newborn king gifts. The world was given a new Savior that day!

Travel Game #16
Star-Crossed Sky-Lines

Player 1 takes out a piece of paper and folds it in half.
Next, Player 1 draws tiny spots, like stars, over half of the page,
anywhere they want (at least 20 stars total).
Then the game goes to the next player,
who draws a line between any two stars on the page.
The next player then takes the paper and connects any two stars he
wishes, but his line cannot cross the line of the first player.
This continues until there are no more lines to be drawn
without crossing another line.
The player who successfully draws the last connecting line,
without crossing any other line on the page, wins!
Players draw spots on the other half of the page and begin again!

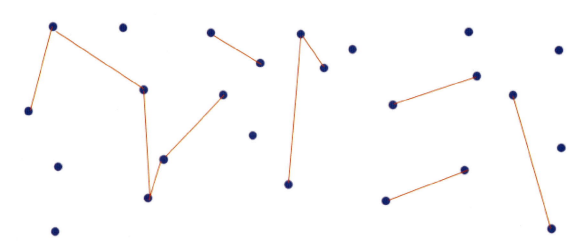

Children, Go Where I Send Thee
CD Track 16

Children, go where I send thee.
How shall I send thee?
I'm gonna send thee 1 by 1,
One for the little bitty baby,
Born, born, born in Bethlehem.

Children, go where I send thee.
How shall I send thee?
I'm gonna send thee 2 by 2,
Two for Paul and Silas,
One for the little bitty baby,
Born, born, born in Bethlehem.

Children, go where I send thee.
How shall I send thee?
I'm gonna send thee 3 by 3,
Three for the Hebrew children,
Two for Paul and Silas,
One for the little bitty baby,
Born, born, born in Bethlehem.

(add one line per verse for seven more verses)

4 for the 4 that stood at the door.

5 for the 5 gospel preachers.

6 for the 6 that never got fixed.

7 for the 7 that never went to heaven.

8 for the 8 that stood at the gate.

9 for the 9 that dressed so fine.

10 for the 10 Commandments.

Be still and know that I am God.
Psalm 46:10

The Boy Jesus

I will go to church

When Jesus was twelve years old, Mary and Joseph made their yearly journey to Jerusalem. There they would celebrate the Passover feast. The feast lasted for several days. When it ended, they began the long journey home. Thinking that Jesus was with his friends, they became worried when Jesus was nowhere to be found.

They hurried back to Jerusalem. To their amazement, they found Jesus in the temple! Mary and Joseph were glad to find him safe. Jesus said, "Didn't you know that I had to be in my Father's house?"

Travel Game #17

The Math Whiz

Don't ask how it works, but it does! Follow the directions below to figure out the secret number of any player!

It helps to have a calculator to do this trick. See if you have a calculator on a cell phone in the car.

Begin by someone choosing a secret number that is less than 100.

Next, ask them their age.

Multiply their age by 2, then add 5.

Multiply this number by 50, then subtract 365.

Have the person with the secret number add their number to the total from the above steps.

Add 115.

The resulting number will give you the person's age and secret number. The last two digits are the person's secret number. The other numbers are their age!

Age x 2 + 5 x 50 - 365 + Secret Number + 115 = Age & Secret Number

Number = 7

Age = 7

Total = 707

J-O-Y
CD Track 17

Joy, joy, j-o-y, oh I will sing of
Joy, joy, j-o-y, oh I will sing.
Make music to the Lord.
I will sacrifice with joy, joy, j-o-y.
Oh my, just shout with joy!

Joy, joy, j-o-y, oh I will sing of
Joy, joy, j-o-y, oh I will sing.
Make music to the Lord.
I will sacrifice with joy, joy, j-o-y.
Oh my, just shout with joy!

Deep down inside
I got a little love I can't hide
Whenever I sing of the Lord.
Down in my heart
I got a little love ready to start
Whenever I sing of the Lord.

I was glad when they said, let us go to the house of the Lord.
Psalm 122:1

The Widow's Mite

I will give my all to Jesus

In the eyes of Jesus, a penny given in love is worth a lot more than a dollar given selfishly. We see this example in a most generous widow. One day Jesus sat in the temple. He listened as the very rich boasted of their giving. They had many coins they put in the money box. They were very proud!

As they continued to talk about themselves, a widow came forward with a tiny offering. She placed two little coins in the box. This was far less than the rich men had given . . . or was it?

Jesus spoke up, "The rich gave a small portion of what they possess. But this widow has given everything she has to God. This is a great sacrifice." It pleases God when we give our all!

Travel Game #18
To the Last Mite!

For 2 players:

In this game, each player starts with 5 coins.
The coins can be of any value. All you need is a "heads" and a "tails."
Each player flips one coin, taking turns guessing how they think
the coins will land when they're flipped. The coins can be either "odd,"
(meaning 1 head and 1 tail) or "even" (meaning 2 heads or 2 tails).
If the player correctly guesses "odds" or "evens,"
the coins that are flipped are added to his stack of coins.
Play continues until one player has collected all of the coins!

For 3 players:

Each player starts with 5 coins.
All three players flip one of their coins.
If the coins are uneven (1 head and 2 tails, or 2 heads and 1 tail),
the player whose coins are different gets to keep all three.
If all three come up the same (3 heads or 3 tails),
all three coins go into the pot and are awarded to the winner of the next flip.
Once a player is out of coins, he is out of the game.
Play then moves to the rules outlined in the "For 2 Players" section above.

The winner is the player who ends up with all of the coins!

J-E-S-U-S
CD Track 18

There is a name I love to sing,
And Jesus is his name-o.
J-E-S-U-S, J-E-S-U-S,
J-E-S-U-S
And Jesus is his name-o.

There is a name I love to sing,
And Jesus is his name-o.
(clap) E-S-U-S, (3x)
And Jesus is his name-o.

There is a name I love to sing,
And Jesus is his name-o.
(clap, clap) S-U-S, (3x)
And Jesus is his name-o.

There is a name I love to sing,
And Jesus is his name-o.
(clap, clap, clap) U-S, (3x)
And Jesus is his name-o.

There is a name I love to sing.
And Jesus is his name-o.
(clap, clap, clap, clap) S, (3x)
And Jesus is his name-o.

There is a name I love to sing,
And Jesus is his name-o.
(clap, clap, clap, clap, clap) (3x)
And Jesus is his name-o.

FREELY you have RECEIVED. FREELY GIVE. MATTHEW 10:8

Jesus & The Children

I will celebrate God's love for me

Do you know why Jesus said we need childlike faith to enter the kingdom of heaven? Children are full of love, ready to trust, and eager to believe. That's childlike faith!

Jesus and his disciples had traveled to Jordan. When they arrived, the people crowded around Jesus. They wanted to hear the good news and be healed. When several people brought children to Jesus, the disciples turned them away.

Is Jesus just for big people? Of course not! Jesus said, "Let the little children come to me. The kingdom of heaven will be full of people who have faith like a child."

The disciples began to understand that Jesus loves everyone, big or small, young or old. He seeks those who are full of love, ready to trust, and eager to believe . . . just like a child!

Travel Game #19
Alphabet Story

Player 1 begins by telling a story,
using the letters of the alphabet in order!
For example: A big cat drove elephants forward.
Go as far as you can.
The next player begins with the next letter.
For example: Green horses in Jackson kept living.
See how far you can go . . . and how wacky you can get!

Under Victoria's X-ray Yo-Yo ...

Do, Do to Others
CD Track 19

Do, do, do, do, do, do, do, do to others,
Do, do, do, do, do, do, do, do to others
What you would have them do to you, to you.
Do, do, do, do what you would have them do to you,
To you, do, do, do, do, do, do, do to others.

If you want people to treat you kind,
Treat them kind.
That's how it goes.
If you want people to treat you kind,
Treat them kind, I say.

For God so loved the world, He gave his only Son.
John 3:16

The Good Samaritan

I will show my love to others

The best way to show the world that you love the Lord is to love others. We see this lesson in the story of the good Samaritan. As a man was traveling from Jerusalem to Jericho, he was attacked by robbers. He lay there beaten and bruised when a priest came by. This was an important priest, perhaps on his way to serve at the temple in Jerusalem. "I am far too important to spend time with this man," he thought. So he passed by. In a while, a second priest came by, but he passed the dying man as well.

Then came a Samaritan from another country. His heart was full of love and compassion for the hurting. When he saw the man, he stopped, bandaged his wounds, and carried him to an inn. Jesus said this is the way we are to treat our neighbors, with love and kindness.

Travel Game #20
A-long the Road

Each player must write the complete alphabet on a piece of paper. The driver of the car declares the game started when driving through an area that has no billboards. Players must cross off each letter of the alphabet from A-Z. In order to cross off a letter, they must find it on a billboard or other roadside sign. The first player to complete the alphabet, A-Z, is the winner!

"The quick brown fox jumps over a lazy dog" is one sentence that uses all 26 letters!

Do Not Judge
CD Track 20

Do not judge
Or you too will be judged.
Do not judge
Or you too will be judged.
Do not judge
Or you too will be judged.
Do not judge
Or you too will be judged.

For in the same way you judge others,
You will be judged,
You will be judged.
And with the measure you use to measure,
It will be measured unto you.

Love your neighbor as you love yourself.
Matthew 22:39

The Woman at the Well
I will treat all people with respect

As you travel, you may meet someone from another country. How should you treat them? The same way Jesus did! He once met a Samaritan woman at a well. Since Jesus was Jewish, she did not expect him to speak to her. But Jesus said, "Will you give me a drink of water?" She was surprised and answered, "I am a Samaritan. You are a Jew. How can you ask me for a drink?"

Jesus said, "I can give you Living Water." She thought, "You don't even have a jar. Where do you get Living Water?"

Jesus knew all about her and shared God's love with her. Jesus told her that he was the Messiah she had hoped for. This turned her sorrow into joy. When we meet someone new, we must look beyond skin color and religious beliefs. We should treat all people as a creation of God.

Travel Game #21

Holes, Ropes, & Buckets

The first player chooses a number between 1-99.
The second player then guesses the number. Here's how:
When Player 2 guesses, the first player must compare that number to his own number, and respond as follows:

If the second player chooses a number that has no matching numbers, they are said to have "holes."

For example: If the first player's number is 15, and the second player says 42, the second player has 2 holes—no matches.

If the second player has digits matching the first player's, but they are not in the right place, they are called "ropes."

For example: If the first player's number is 15, and the second player says 51, all of his numbers are ropes.

If the second player has digits matching the first player's, and they are in the right place, they are called "buckets."

If the first player's number is 15, and the second player says 12, they have 1 bucket (and 1 hole), because 1 of the numbers is right and in the right place.

The first player must tell the second how many buckets, ropes, and holes the second player has. The game continues until the second player guesses the first player's number.

Players go for 3 rounds. The player who guesses the other's number in the fewest total guesses between the three rounds wins!

The Lord Is My Shepherd
CD Track 21

The Lord is, the Lord is my shepherd.
The Lord is, the Lord is my shepherd.
I shall not be in want.
The Lord is, the Lord is my shepherd.
The Lord is, the Lord is my shepherd.
I shall not be in want.
The Lord is my shepherd,
I shall not be in want.

He leads me beside still waters.
He restores my soul.
He makes me lie down in green pastures.
He restores my soul.

Show proper respect to everyone you meet.
1 Peter 2:17

ONE LOST SHEEP
I will tell others about the Lord

Jesus loved to speak in parables. Parables are little short stories that teach a great big lesson. In this parable, Jesus told of a little lamb that had wandered away from the flock. What does a good shepherd do? He leaves the flock of sheep in the meadow. Then he looks until he finds the lost lamb. And when he finds the lamb, the shepherd is so happy! He calls his friends and says, "Come celebrate with me, for I have found the little lost lamb!"

Jesus said it is that way in heaven. There is more celebration when one lost person comes to the Lord than over 99 who do not need to repent. And the great big lesson of this parable is that we are like shepherds searching for lost lambs. So let's go out and bring them to the Lord!

Travel Game #22
I Spy (Your Sheep)

First, one person looks around them in the car and finds something that they think will be hard to guess. They then say "I spy something . . ." and then describe that thing. So if mom is wearing green earrings, and that is the thing the first player spied, he would say, "I spy something green." Then each player must make a guess at what the thing was. Everyone playing gets one turn making a guess. If no one guesses the item correctly in the first round, a second round follows. But in this round, each player gets to ask a question about the item, like, "Is it something you can eat," or "Is it in the front seat or the back seat?" There can be no guessing in this round. Every player gets to ask one question. Players then take another round guessing what the item was. Rounds alternate like this until the item is correctly guessed. The one who guesses correctly is the winner!

Believe It, Receive It
CD Track 22

Whatever you ask for in prayer
Believe it now
Whatever you ask for in prayer
Whatever you ask for in prayer
Believe it now
Whatever you ask for in prayer
Only believe that you have received it
And it will be yours
Whatever you ask for in prayer
Believe it now, and receive it too!

You need faith, just believe it now,
You need hope, come receive it now,
You need love, just believe it now,
And it will be yours.

You need health, just believe it now,
You need joy, come receive it now,
You need peace, just believe it now,
And it will be yours.

They Preached The Good News!
Acts 14:21

A Sick Man Believes
I will take a small step of faith

Is your faith growing? Faith is believing and then acting upon the promises of God. A very sick man once demonstrated a great faith! Jesus and his twelve disciples were traveling through Galilee. They had healed many people. One day, a man came to Jesus with sores all over his body. He believed Jesus could heal him. He acted on his faith and called to Jesus, "I know you can heal me, if you are willing." Jesus rejoiced at hearing such faith! "I am willing," he said. And the man was healed.

God has made so many wonderful promises. Let's believe God and take a small step of faith today!

Travel Game #23
Billboard Madness!

This game is easy and simple. Pretend to be whatever appears on the next billboard. If it's an ad for an alligator farm, then you pretend to be an alligator. If it's an ad for breakfast sandwiches, pretend to be sizzling bacon!

The second player begins when the next billboard is passed. Everyone will continue to pretend until the car is full of alligators and sizzling bacon . . . or whatever you see!

I'm a piece of bacon!

Deep and Wide
CD Track 23

Deep and wide, deep and wide,
There's a fountain flowing deep and wide.
Deep and wide, deep and wide,
There's a fountain flowing deep and wide.

(clap) and wide, (clap) and wide,
There's a fountain flowing (clap) and wide.
(clap) and wide, (clap) and wide,
There's a fountain flowing (clap) and wide.

(clap) and (clap), (clap) and (clap),
There's a fountain flowing (clap) and (clap).
(clap) and (clap), (clap) and (clap),
There's a fountain flowing (clap) and (clap).

(clap) and (clap), (clap) and (clap),
There's a (clap) flowing (clap) and (clap).
Deep and wide, deep and wide,
There's a fountain flowing deep and wide.

The Righteous shall live by faith.
Romans 1:17

The Prodigal Son

I will be thankful for God's love

Do you know why Jesus called his followers "disciples" and not "the fun company"? Because those who follow Jesus must show discipline. Once there was a man who had two sons. One was very disciplined. But the other one decided to leave his father and join the "wild crowd." He asked for his share of his father's possessions and left. He was not disciplined. He wasted every penny on things that would displease his father. One morning, he woke up in a pig pen, poor and alone. He thought, "I'm sorry I did this. I'll go home. I'll ask my father if I can be his servant."

On returning home, he learned the meaning of a father's love. As he approached the house, his father was watching for him. He ran to his child and kissed him before he ever said a word. That kiss said, "I love you, I forgive you. You are still my son!"

Travel Game #24

Who Knows Best?

This game is a trivia contest between teams.
First, divide into two teams.
The first team then looks through this book and finds a fact, tidbit, or anything else they can ask a question about.
The second team must answer the question. If they get it right, they get a point. They also get asked another question.
When the team being asked the question gets it wrong, the teams switch. The team that asked the question now answers, and the team that answered now asks.
First team to get 7 questions right is the winner!

What questions will your team ask?

The Beauty of the Lord
CD Track 24

May the beauty of the Lord be upon us.
May the beauty of the Lord be upon us.

And may they see Christ live in me
And come to see his face.
And may they find my life entwined
With his amazing grace.

May the beauty of the Lord be upon us.
May the beauty of the Lord be upon us.

And may they see thy majesty
In all we do and say.
And may they know God loves them so
And find his perfect way.

Let us be thankful and so worship God.
Hebrews 12:28

Jesus Heals

I will be thankful for all God has done

We should always remember to thank those who help us. One day, ten lepers met Jesus on the road to Jerusalem. They cried out to Jesus, "Jesus, have mercy and heal us!" When Jesus saw them, he said, "Go, show yourselves to the priest." They all started walking toward the temple. And as they went, they were healed.

Still, only one of the ten came back to thank Jesus. Let us all be thankful for the love and health Jesus gives to us!

Travel Game #25
Countin' Cows for Miles

This one is really easy!
Divide the car up into left and right.
Now you're going to count the cows you see!
The driver selects a distance (10 miles for example).
The team that counts the most cows on their side of the car in the set distance (10 miles) is the winner!

How many cows did you count?

Cast Your Cares
CD Track 25

Cast your cares on the Lord.
He will sustain you.
He will never let the righteous fall.
Cast your cares on the Lord.
He will sustain you.
He will never let the righteous fall.

We get so troubled,
Pressure is doubled.
God seems far away.
When storm clouds gather
I'd really rather
Cast my cares—pray, oh pray, oh pray!

Cast your cares on the Lord.
He will sustain you.
He will never let the righteous fall.
Cast your cares on the Lord.
He will sustain you.
He will never let the righteous fall.

Since we have such hope, we are very bold.
2 Corinthians 3:12

The Blind Man Sees

I will show kindness and mercy

Kindness and mercy are two very special words. Kindness means showing love to everyone. Mercy means showing love to those who may not deserve it.

Once a blind man called out, "Jesus, son of David, have mercy on me!" This happened in the city of Jericho as a blind man sat by the roadside. His name was Bartimaeus. "Jesus," he shouted again, "I need your help!"

Jesus asked him what he wanted. "I want to see again," Bartimaeus pleaded. Jesus showed the blind man mercy. He said, "Go and be healed." Suddenly, Bartimaeus could see the sky, the trees, the clouds—and he could see Jesus. What mercy Jesus showed!

Travel Game #26

Honey, I Love You . . .

Player 1 begins the game by turning to the person next to him and saying, "Honey, if you love me, you'd smile." The person Player 1 was speaking to must respond with, "Honey, I love you, but I just can't smile." The trick is, you have to say it without cracking even the slightest of grins! If you smile when you're responding, you're out. The last player in the game is the winner.

Honey, I love you, but I just can't smile!

Love Your Neighbor
CD Track 26

Love, love la-la-la-la-la love
Your neighbor as yourself.
Love, love la-la-la-la-la love
Your neighbor as yourself.

We gotta show a little kindness,
(show a little kindness)
Show the world we really care.
Let the love of Jesus find us
(love of Jesus find us)
Singing his love everywhere.

Love, love la-la-la-la-la love
Your neighbor as yourself.
Love, love la-la-la-la-la love
Your neighbor as yourself.

We gotta share the love of Jesus,
(share the love of Jesus)
Share it with everyone.
And may everyone who sees us
(everyone who sees us)
Open their hearts
And love the Son.

Be merciful, just as your Father is merciful. Luke 6:36

A Boy Lives Again

I will think about heaven

The Bible teaches that death is not the end. Because Jesus came, not even the sadness and loss of death must go on forever. And because he cares for you, he will be there to help you no matter how upset you may be. The Bible also tells us that if you believe in Jesus, you will live forever with him in heaven.

Once in the town of Nain, Jesus met some very sad people. A funeral was passing by. A small child had died and his mother was weeping. Jesus could see in the mother's tears a great love and a broken heart. His compassion overflowed as he reached out and touched the coffin. Everyone stopped.

"Young boy," he commanded, "get up!" To the utter joy and amazement of all, the boy sat up. He was alive! His mother shouted with joy. Everyone was so happy that the young boy was alive again!

Travel Game #27
Cows & the Barnyard

Divide up into teams, the right side of the car and the left. Each team must look for cows on the side of the road and count as many as they can. They receive one point for each cow they see on their side of the car.

However, when a barn appears on one side of the road, the team on that side loses all their cows and starts all over again.

Play may last for a certain time (30-60 minutes), number of miles (30-40) or a certain number of cows (101).

Find a barn, lose your cows!

I Will Sing of the Mercies
CD Track 27

I will sing of the mercies of the Lord forever.
I will sing, I will sing.
I will sing of the mercies of the Lord forever.
I will sing of the mercies of the Lord.

With my mouth will I make known
Thy faithfulness, thy faithfulness.
With my mouth will I make known
Thy faithfulness to all generations.

I will sing of the mercies of the Lord forever.
I will sing, I will sing.
I will sing of the mercies of the Lord forever.
I will sing of the mercies of the Lord.

Set your heart on things above.
Colossians 3:1

The Rooftop Miracle
I will bring my friends to Jesus

We should always tell our friends about Jesus. The Bible tells us about four men who wanted their friend to see Jesus.

Jesus had traveled from Galilee to Capernaum. On this day, Jesus was teaching in a home. Four men had brought their sick friend to Jesus. They knew Jesus could heal him. But it was too crowded to get in the door. Still, they didn't let that stop them. They cut a big hole in the roof and lowered their friend down until he was right before Jesus.

What great love and faith the four friends showed! Jesus said to the sick man, "Stand up! Take your mat and go." The man was healed right away. All the people were amazed—not only that Jesus healed the man, but at the boldness his friends showed in taking him to see Jesus.

Travel Game #28
Rooftop Dot Game!

Here's a great game for long road trips:
First, grab a piece of paper.
Then **TRACE** the dots to the left onto your page.
Each player gets to connect any two of the
dots with a line.
Whoever closes up a triangle gets to put their initial in the triangle, like it is right here

The one with the most triangles when all lines have been drawn is the winner!

FOR MORE FUN,
MAKE THE TRIANGLE BIGGER
BY ADDING MORE ROWS OF DOTS!

Is Anything Too Hard for the Lord
CD Track 28

Is anything too hard for the Lord?
Is anything too hard for the Lord?
There is nothing he can't do.
Have a little faith, believe it's true,
And you will find there's nothing he can't do.

Can He part a sea? (Yes, he can!)
Make the blind to see? (Yes, he can!)
Walk on water? (Yes, he can!)
Pray to the Father? (Yes, he can!)
Nothing too big, nothing too small.
Nothing he can't do at all.
There's nothing, nothing, nothing,
Nothing he can't do.

Since we have such hope,
we are very bold.
2 Corinthians 4:12

Lazarus, Come Forth!
I will call Jesus my friend

If you love Jesus and call him friend, you will live forever. Lazarus found this to be true!

Lazarus was a friend of Jesus. And Jesus loved Lazarus very much. One day, Jesus was told that Lazarus was very ill. But Jesus waited two days before he went to Lazarus. By the time Jesus got there, his friend had died. Lazarus had a sister named Mary. She was heartbroken. "Why didn't you come?" Mary asked. "If you had been here, he wouldn't have died." Jesus wept. "Take me to the tomb," he said.

Jesus stood before the tomb and shouted, "Lazarus, come out of there!" Out came Lazarus, alive! Who is this man who heals the sick and gives life to the dead? His name is Jesus. He is my friend!

Travel Game #29

Letter Chains

Player 1 starts by naming any object he wishes.
For example, he might say, "Airplane."
Player 2 must say an object that starts with the
last letter of the word Player 1 said.
So he would say something like, "Elephant."
Player 3 would say something that begins
with the last letter of that word.
The game goes on until the objects are so silly that
everyone has to laugh!

This sounds silly!

Let Everything That Has Breath
CD Track 29

Let everything, everything that has breath,
Let everything, everything that has breath,
Praise the Lord, praise the Lord with me
'Til all the world can see
He's a great and mighty God,
So where'er your feet may trod,
Praise the Lord.

Let everything, everything that has breath,
Let everything, everything that has breath,
Praise the Lord, praise the Lord, I say!
Can you hear me today?
Come on, every girl and boy,
Make a mighty noise and praise the Lord!

A FRIEND LOVES AT ALL TIMES.
PROVERBS 17:17

The Feeding of 5,000
I will give to those in need

A little in the hands of Jesus is worth so much more than a lot in our own.

It was late in the evening when the disciples said to Jesus, "Send the crowds away so they may eat." But to their surprise, Jesus said, "You feed them." They said, "There are 5,000 people here! How can we feed them?"

Then Andrew said, "There is a boy here with five loaves of bread and two fish." He looked at Jesus and asked, "How far will that go?"

Jesus took the loaves of bread and the fish and said a prayer. Then he began to break the loaves and fish into pieces. 5,000 people were fed that day. And after everyone had eaten, the disciples gathered twelve baskets of food. That's how far a small lunch can go! A little given to Jesus can do a lot!

Travel Game #30
The Picnic Basket

A B C D E F G H I J K L M N O P Q R S T U V W X Y Z

A boy gave Jesus his lunch, and Jesus fed thousands of people with it! Now it's your turn to pack lunch! Or at least think of the wackiest picnic basket ever!

First, choose a player to write down answers.

Player 1 starts by saying, "In my picnic basket I packed a …" and saying a food item that begins with "A" (such as apple).

The next person says, "In my picnic basket I packed a …" and repeats player one's "A" word. That player then adds a food item that begins with "B." So he might say, "In my picnic basket I packed an apple and a buffalo wing."

The next player repeats and adds a "C" word, etc.

If a person cannot remember the correct food item for any letter, that player is out. The person to get furthest through the alphabet without making a mistake is the winner!

Loaves & Fishes Song
CD Track 30

Jesus took the five little loaves,
Then Jesus took the two little fish,
Then looking up to heaven,
He gave thanks, he gave thanks.
Looking up to heaven, he gave thanks.

Five thousand were fed with five little loaves.
Five thousand were fed with two little fish.
Then looking up to heaven,
He gave thanks, he gave thanks.
Looking up to heaven, he gave thanks.

Jesus took the five little loaves,
Then Jesus took the two little fish,
Then looking up to heaven,
He gave thanks, he gave thanks.
Looking up to heaven, he gave thanks.

Give and it will be given to you.
Luke 6:38

HUMBLE JESUS
I will show humility

Feet can be funny things. We can wiggle our toes and tickle them until we laugh out loud. But Jesus used them to teach a lesson of humility.

Just before the Passover feast, Jesus gathered the disciples. He had already taught them that to be a great Christian, you must humble yourself and become like a servant. You must favor others above yourself.

So Jesus, the son of Almighty God, filled a bowl with water. Then he took a cloth and began to wash the feet of his disciples. It was his way of showing them how to be humble.

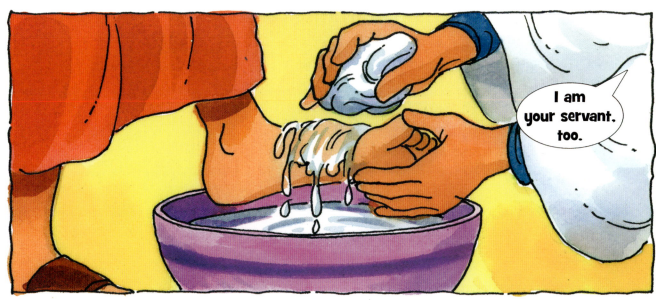

Travel Game #31
Air Verses

Player 1—think of a word, any word!
Player 2 then closes his eyes and holds out his hand.
Player 1 uses his finger to "write" the
word on the other person's hand.
See if you can figure out what word the other person is writing!

Put out your hand!

Amazing Grace / Jesus Loves Me
CD Track 31

Amazing grace, how sweet the sound
That saved a wretch like me.
I once was lost but now am found,
Was blind but now I see.

'Twas grace that taught
My heart to fear
And grace my fears relieved.
How precious did that grace appear
The hour I first believed.

Jesus, save this heart of mine,
Make it pure and wholly thine.
On the cross you died for me.
I will try to live for thee.

Yes, Jesus loves me
Yes, Jesus loves me
Yes, Jesus loves me
The Bible tells me so.

When we've been there
Ten thousand years,
Bright shining as the sun,
We've no less days
To sing God's praise
Than when we first begun.

We've no less days
To sing God's praise
Than when we first begun.

Show true humility to all men. Titus 3:2

JESUS IS ARRESTED
I will go where God leads me

Are you willing to go wherever God wants you to go? Jesus took Peter, James, and John to a quiet place to pray. In the garden of Gethsemane, he asked them to stay awake and watch. Then Jesus walked a few steps further and prayed, "Father, I am willing to do what you want, not what I want." Three times Jesus returned to find the disciples sleeping.

Then out from the darkness came Judas, the betrayer. Judas stood before Jesus and kissed him, saying, "Master." This kiss let the guards know which one to arrest. They grabbed Jesus and arrested him.

He was taken to Caiaphas the high priest. Jesus told Caiaphas that he was, indeed, the Son of God. Caiaphas pronounced him guilty and sent him to Pilate. Yes, Jesus was willing to go to the cross for you and me. He was willing to go wherever God wanted him to go . . . are you?

Travel Game #32
Nothing Missed

At the bottom of this page you'll find several lists of things to watch for as you're traveling.
First, choose a list.
Then, everyone who wants to play copies the list onto their own paper.
The first one to find everything on their list (it can be, for example, a real horse, or a horse on a billboard) is the winner!
If you use up all of the lists below, make up your own!

Pick which list of things you are going to look for!

List #1	List #2	List #3	List #4	List #5	List #6
Dog	Cow	Horse	Cat	A Deer	Bird
Barn	House	Red Car	Truck	Yellow	Graveyard
Airplane	Man	Boy	Girl	Sign	Tractor
Truck	Tree	Lake	Boat	Woman	Fence
The Number "2"	Train	Stop Sign	Hill	River	Mall
A Speed Limit Sign	Guard Rail	Motorcycle	Bus	Parking Lot	Sidewalk
	The Letter "A"	The Number "3"	The Letter "B"	Picnic Table	The Letter "C"
				The Number "4"	

The Lord's Prayer
CD Track 32

Our Father in heaven,
Hallowed be your name.
Our Father in heaven,
Hallowed be your name.

Your kingdom come,
Your will be done
On earth as it is in heaven.
Your kingdom come,
Your will be done
On earth as it is in heaven.

Our Father in heaven,
Hallowed be your name.
Our Father in heaven,
Hallowed be your name.

Give us today our daily bread.
Forgive us our debts
As we also have
Forgiven our debtors.

Our Father in heaven,
Hallowed be your name.
Our Father in heaven,
Hallowed be your name.

And lead us not into temptation
But deliver us from evil.
For yours is the kingdom
And the power and the glory
Forever and ever.

Our Father in heaven,
Hallowed be your name.
Our Father in heaven,
Hallowed be your name.

He leads me along the right paths. Psalm 23:3

Peter Denies Jesus
I will remember God forgives

Sometimes we want to do the right thing. But in a moment of weakness, we fail. Even the apostle Peter had a great failure in his life. But God forgave him.

Just before going to the Mount of Olives, Jesus told the twelve disciples that one of them would betray him. Peter spoke up to say he would never deny Jesus, no matter what.

Perhaps his intentions were good, but Jesus answered, "Before the rooster crows in the morning, you will deny me three times."

That night, Jesus was arrested and beaten as Peter stood outside. Three people approached Peter and said, "You were with Jesus!" Peter said, "No, I wasn't with him. I don't know Jesus." When he heard the rooster crow, he remembered what Jesus had said. He was very sorry and wept bitterly.

Jesus forgave Peter. He will forgive us, too.

Travel Game #33
Three Times

Player 1 starts by saying something he's done three times today. Player 2 then responds with something <u>he's</u> done three times today. Go around the car and see what everyone has done three times. If you can't think of anything you've done three times—without repeating something someone else has said—you're out. The last player remaining is the winner!

Have you played this game 3 times today?

I Am the Good Shepherd
CD Track 33

I am the good shepherd
I am the good shepherd
And the good shepherd
Lays down his life
For the sheep.
I am the good shepherd
I am the good shepherd
And the good shepherd
Lays down his life
For the sheep.
'Cause he loves them,
He loves them,
Oh how he loves each one.
He loves them, he loves them,
Like a shepherd
He'll lead me home.

Jesus is the good shepherd
Jesus is the good shepherd
And the good shepherd
Lays down his life
For the sheep.
Jesus is the good shepherd
Jesus is the good shepherd
And the good shepherd
Lays down his life
For the sheep.
'Cause he loves them,
He loves them,
Oh how he loves each one.
He loves them, he loves them,
For Jesus will lead me home,
Lead me home.

The Lord forgives all your sins.
Psalm 103:3

The Crucifixion

I will remember Christ died for me

To sacrifice is to give up something we have for someone else. Jesus made the biggest sacrifice. He gave his life for you and me.

God's plan to save us from our sin meant that Jesus would die on a cross. As Jesus made his way down the road to Calvary, he was very tired. The cross was heavy. A man named Simon carried the cross the rest of the way.

Then the Roman soldiers put nails in Jesus' hands and feet as they nailed him to the cross. What a sacrifice Jesus made!

To die for another is the ultimate sacrifice. There on Calvary, Jesus died for you and me.

Travel Game #34

Car-i-oke

Take out your "Ultimate Travel Time" CD
and pop it into the CD player.
Then you become the star!
Each person in the car takes turns singing
one of the songs . . . all by themselves!
Don't be shy! You could be the next superstar!
And remember, the lyrics to every song are printed in this book.

You sing very well!

My Grace Is Sufficient
CD Track 34

My grace is sufficient for you, for you.
My grace is sufficient for you, for you.
My grace is sufficient for you, for you.
My grace is sufficient for you, for you.

For my mercy is made perfect
In weakness, in weakness.
For my mercy is made perfect
Just speak this, oh speak this.

While we were still sinners, Christ died for us.
Romans 5:8

The Believers Share

I will share what I have with others

What we learn in Sunday school is sometimes forgotten as we get older—things like "share with others." The early Christians taught us a great lesson in sharing.

After Jesus ascended into heaven, the first Christian church began. These early Christians believed in sharing what God had given to them. They were happy to share their homes and property with other believers.

Joseph of Cyprus was a man who believed and practiced the good habit of sharing. He sold the land God had given to him and gave the money to the disciples. Christians should always share with others, especially other believers.

Travel Game #35

The Animal Game

Player 1 thinks of an animal—but don't tell anyone what it is.
Then player 1 tells the others the first and last letter of the animal
(if their animal is <u>s</u>quirre<u>l</u>, for example, you'd say "<u>S</u>, <u>L</u>")
The other players must guess the name of the animal.
The first one to guess three correctly wins!

Is your animal a <u>d</u>uc<u>k</u>?

Crown Him with Many Crowns
CD Track 35

Crown him with many crowns,
The Lamb upon his throne.
Hark, how the heavenly
Anthem drowns
All music but its own.
Awake, my soul and sing
Of him who died for thee
And hail him as thy matchless King
Through all eternity.

Crown him the Lord of love.
Behold his hands and side,
Rich wounds yet visible above
In beauty glorified.
No angel in the sky
Can fully bear that sight,
But downward bends
His wondering eye
At mysteries so bright.

Crown him the Lord of life
Who triumphed o'er the grave,
Who rose victorious to the strife
For those he came to save.
His glories now we sing
Who died and rose on high,
Who died eternal life to bring
And lives that death may die.

Who died eternal life to bring
And lives that death may die.
Amen!

SHARE WITH THOSE IN NEED.
Romans 12:13

A Crippled Man Walks
I will ask God for things big and small

The Bible says, "Ask and you will receive." But sometimes we ask so little because we think our God is small. A crippled man did just that!

One day Peter and John were on their way to the temple. There by the gate sat a crippled man. "Please give me some money," he begged.

The two disciples told the beggar that they had no silver or gold, but what they did have was much better. They called upon the name of Jesus for healing. Suddenly, the man stood up! His legs were strong!

Together, the three men walked into the temple, praising God all the way. Yes, our God is big enough to handle anything you can ask for. So ask big!

Travel Game #36

Finger Walk

Open your "Travel Time Bible" to any page.
Close your eyes, then point to a word.
Open your eyes.
Now give the other players clues so they can guess your word.
Keep track of how many clues it takes to guess the secret word.
The one who guesses your word given the fewest clues wins!

What was your secret word?

No Other Name
CD Track 36

There is no other name under heaven
Given to men by which we must be saved.
Oh, there is no other name,
There is no other name under heaven,
There is no other name.
Only Jesus, only Jesus can save a wayward soul.
Only Jesus, only Jesus can make a sinner whole.
His name can make the blind to see,
Give you hope, oh I believe,
Only Jesus can save a wayward soul.

Ask and it will be given to you.
Matthew 7:7

Lydia Learns a Lesson
I will tell my family about God's love

Telling others about God's love is an important part of being a believer. This was true in the life of Lydia.

Lydia was a successful business woman who lived near Macedonia. She sold purple cloth. One Sabbath day, Lydia was down by the river, just outside the city gate. There many women had gathered. On that same day, Paul the missionary had come to the river to find a quiet place to pray.

The women met Paul, and upon hearing Paul's message, Lydia became a believer. She told her family about Jesus, too. Lydia opened up her home to Paul and those traveling with him. She became the first person in all of Europe to believe in Jesus!

Travel Game #37
Purple Boardgame

Lydia wants to give her best purple garment to Paul, but she needs your help to get there! Each player picks a color. Flip a coin to move—1 space for heads, 2 spaces for tails. If you land on your own color, you can flip again. But do what the space you land on says to do, no matter what color you are!

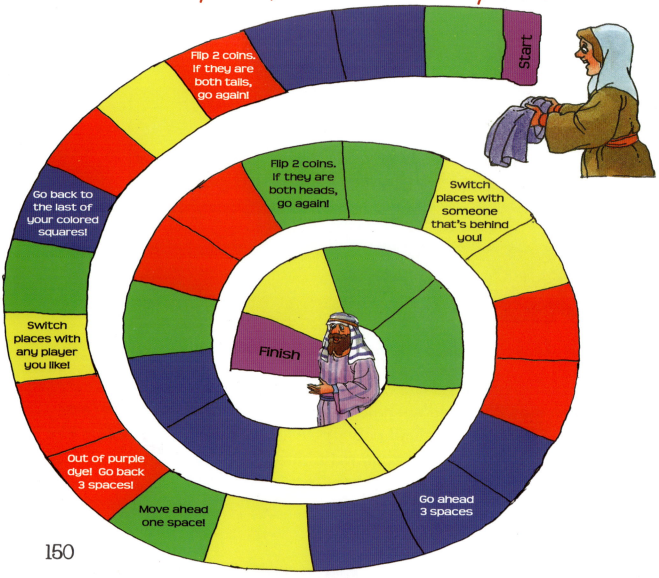

150

Come and See
CD Track 37

I will praise you with my whole heart.
I will praise you with my song.
I will praise you in the morning
Before the dawn comes to call.

Come and see the mercy of the Lord.
Come and share his grace.
Come and see the mercy of the Lord
And give him praise,
Not to last a week or year
But all your days.

I will praise you with my whole heart.
I will praise you with my song.
I will praise you in the morning
Before the dawn comes to call.

In the beginning, God created the heavens and the earth.
Genesis 1:1

Dorcas Awakes
I will be generous to the poor

Dorcas was a generous, kindhearted woman who lived in the city of Joppa. Her unselfish deeds were known by all. She shared everything she had with the poor.

One day, Dorcas became very sick and died. One of her friends ran to get Peter, a disciple of Jesus. "Please come with us. Dorcas has died!" they shouted. When Peter arrived, he was taken to where Dorcas lay. He prayed, then said, "Dorcas, get up!"

Dorcas opened her eyes and sat up! Many people came to know the Lord because of her kindness and generosity.

Travel Game #38

Fortunately/Unfortunately

Always look on the bright side! That's what this game is about!
First, one person says something unfortunate, like
"Unfortunately, there's a lion in the car."
The next player says,
"Fortunately, he's not driving."
The next player says,
"Unfortunately, he's hungry."
Then, "Fortunately, he only eats pizza."
Then, "Unfortunately, he thinks YOU are a pizza."
You get the picture! The game goes until everyone laughs!

Fortunately we have all of these games to play!

Come to Me
CD Track 38

Come to me, O come to me
All you who are weary.
Come to me, O come to me
All you who are burdened.
And I will give you rest,
I will give you rest,
I will give you rest.

When the burden seems unbearable
What can you do?
You need a friend to come
And help you through.
I have found a friend in Jesus,
So faithful and true,
And the promise that he made I sing to you.

A generous person will be blessed.
Proverbs 22:9

Paul's Journeys
I will tell others the good news

Missionaries have one purpose. They tell others the good news of God's love for everyone. Perhaps the greatest of all missionaries was Paul the apostle. As he traveled the world, he would tell everyone how he met Jesus on the Damascus Road. Paul was a heart-stirring preacher.

Of the 27 books in the New Testament, Paul wrote 14 of them. Most were letters to the churches of his day. He traveled from Corinth to Ephesus, from Ephesus to Philippi, and throughout the Middle East. From Antioch to Rome, Paul told everyone along the way that God loves them . . . and that he can change your life!

Travel Game #39

Hug Bugs

This game is not for the shy!
When anyone sees a VW Bug come into view,
the first person to see it shouts "Hug Bug!"
That person gets to give a hug to the person
sitting next to them in the car.
Don't unfasten your seatbelt!
(You can always hold your hugs
until the next bathroom break!)

Take a hug, leave a hug!

Go Into All the World
CD Track 39

Go into all the world
And preach the good news to all creation.
Go into all the world
And preach the good news to everyone.

In America? Preach the good news.
In Africa? Preach the good news.
If I go to Mexico? Let them know.
Tell all the world God loves them so.

Go into all the world
And preach the good news to all creation.
Go into all the world
And preach the good news to everyone.

In Asia, too? Preach the good news.
In Australia? Preach the good news.
How about in Morocco? Let them know.
Tell all the world God loves them so.

In Canada? In Japan?
In Chile? In South Africa?

I MUST PREACH THE GOOD NEWS.
LUKE 4:43

The Jailhouse Rocks
I know prayer changes things

A prayer is very powerful. It changes things. Paul and Silas traveled together as missionaries. They helped and healed many people along the way. While in Philippi, they met a young girl who was very troubled. In the name of Jesus, they rid her soul of a bad spirit. Everyone rejoiced. But her guardians were angry. They sent guards to arrest Paul and Silas.

The guards did not believe in Jesus. They beat Paul and Silas and threw them into a cold, dark prison. But even though they were in chains, Paul and Silas sang. They prayed for a miraculous rescue.

Suddenly, an earthquake shook the jail. The chains broke and the doors opened. Paul and Silas were free! The prison guard now knew that Paul's God is a mighty God. He and his family believed and were saved!

Travel Game #40
Paper, Rock, Scissors

Put one hand out, palm down flat, fingers extended—that's paper!
Hold out your hand while making a fist—that's rock!
Stick out your pointer and middle finger—that's scissors!

This game is quick and easy. Are you ready?
Two players, at the same time, make a fist and
pound it on their other hand. One, two, three . . . go!
Then they make their hands form one of the three things above:
Paper, Rock, or Scissors.
Paper beats Rock.
Rock beats Scissors.
Scissors beat Paper.
First player to win three rounds wins the game!

Watch out for trusty Rock!

The Lord Is My Rock
CD Track 40

I love you, O Lord, my strength, my redeemer.
I love you, O Lord, my fortress, my all.
I love you, O Lord, my strength, my redeemer.
So thankful you hear me call

Oh, the Lord is my rock, I will roll to him.
Time and again, he has helped me through.
Oh, the Lord is my rock on whom I depend.
He's the rock, you can roll to him.

When trouble comes, you can roll to him.
Your busted bubble comes, roll to him.
When bad news breaks, you can roll to him.
He is your closest friend.

The prayer of a righteous man is powerful. James 5:16

Stories You'll Read

The Creation	2
Adam & Eve	6
Noah's Ark	10
Joseph's Coat	14
Moses' Burning Bush	18
The Red Sea Miracle	22
Samson's Strength	26
Ruth & Naomi	32
David & Goliath	36
Elijah's Test	40
The 8 Year Old King	44
Queen Esther	48
The Fiery Furnace	52
Daniel and the Lions	56
A Whale of a Tale	60
The Birth of Jesus	64
The Boy Jesus	68
The Widow's Mite	72
Jesus & The Children	76
The Good Samaritan	80

The Woman at the Well	84
One Lost Sheep	88
A Sick Man Believes	92
The Prodigal Son	96
Jesus Heals	100
The Blind Man Sees	104
A Boy Lives Again	108
The Rooftop Miracle	112
Lazarus, Come Forth	116
The Feeding of 5,000	120
Humble Jesus	124
Jesus Is Arrested	128
Peter Denies Jesus	132
The Crucifixion	136
The Believers Share	140
A Crippled Man Walks	144
Lydia Learns a Lesson	148
Dorcas Awakes	152
Paul's Journeys	156
The Jailhouse Rocks	160

Games You'll Play

21 Questions	4
Eden, A to Z	8
Livin' on the Ark	12
Stories by Us	16
Oops Words	20
Red, Yellow, Green	24
Samson's Adventures	28
Smiley Face	34
Travel Time Rhymes	38
The Spelling Test	42
The Rule of 8	46
Esther's Plates	50
Be a Hero	54
Daniel Didn't Drive	58
The Truth in the Tail	62
Star-Crossed Sky-lines	66
The Math Whiz	70
To the Last Mite	74
Alphabet Story	78
A-long the Road	82

Holes, Ropes, & Buckets	86
I Spy (Your Sheep)	90
Billboard Madness	94
Who Knows Best	98
Countin' Cows for Miles	102
Honey, I Love You . . .	106
Cows & The Barnyard	110
Rooftop Dot Game	114
Letter Chains	118
The Picnic Basket	122
Air Verses	126
Nothing Missed	130
Three Times	134
Car-i-oke	138
The Animal Game	142
Finger Walk	146
Purple Boardgame	150
Fortunately/Unfortunately	154
Hug Bugs	158
Paper, Rock, Scissors	162

Songs You'll Sing

	CD	PAGE
In the Beginning	1	5
I Am Wonderfully Made	2	9
Rainbows	3	13
Brother, Where Art Thou	4	17
When I Am Afraid	5	21
I Will Sing to the Lord	6	25
God Is Our Refuge and Strength	7	29
Where You Go	8	35
Be Thou Exalted	9	39
Glorify the Lord with Me	10	43
Because You Are Young	11	47
How Excellent Is Thy Name	12	51
The Plans I Have for You	13	55
Three Times a Day	14	59
Swim, Jonah, Swim	15	63
Children Go Where I Send Thee	16	67
J-O-Y	17	71
J-E-S-U-S	18	75
Do, Do to Others	19	79
Do Not Judge	20	83

	CD	PAGE
The Lord Is My Shepherd	21	87
Believe It, Receive It	22	91
Deep and Wide	23	95
The Beauty of the Lord	24	99
Cast Your Cares	25	103
Love Your Neighbor	26	107
I Will Sing of the Mercies	27	111
Is Anything Too Hard for the Lord	28	115
Let Everything That Has Breath	29	119
Loaves & Fishes Song	30	123
Amazing Grace / Jesus Loves Me	31	127
The Lord's Prayer	32	131
I Am the Good Shepherd	33	135
My Grace Is Sufficient	34	139
Crown Him with Many Crowns	35	143
No Other Name	36	147
Come and See	37	151
Come to Me	38	155
Go into All the World	39	159
The Lord Is My Rock	40	163

I WILL REMEMBER MY CREATOR

GOD CAN DO ALL THINGS!

I WILL SING TO HIM!

TRUST IN GOD!

CELEBRATE GOD'S LOVE!

Do Not Judge!

Magnify His Precious Name!

I Will Remember My Creator

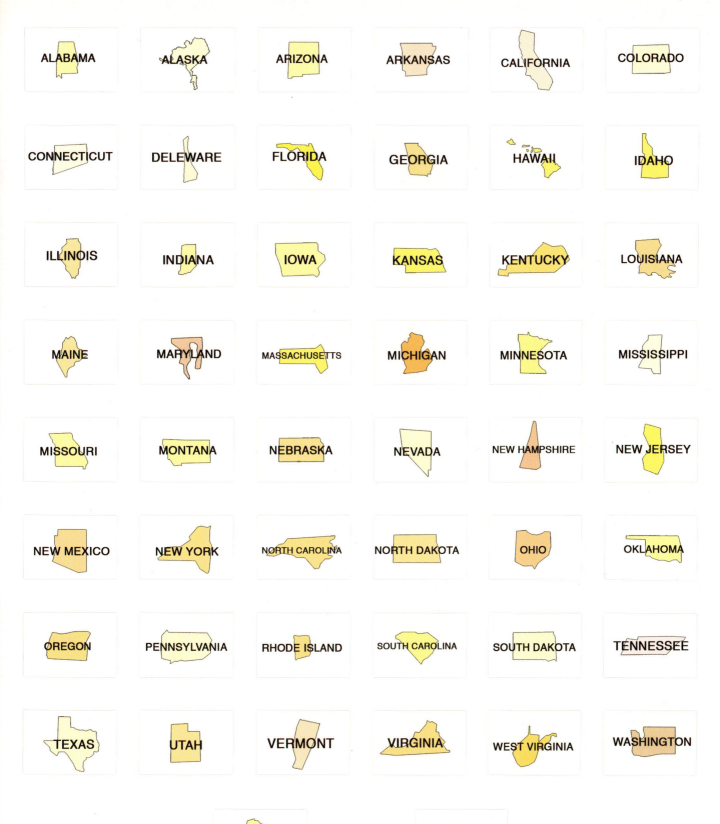